Linking art to the world around us

# artyfacts

# Machines and Transport

Abbey

**CONCEPT**

**Publisher:** Felicia Law

**Design:** Tracy Carrington

**Editorial Planning:** Karen Foster

**Research and Development:** Gerry Bailey, Alec Edgington

**PROJECT DEVELOPMENT**

**Project Director:** Karen Foster

**Editors:** Claire Sipi, Hazel Songhurst, Samantha Sweeney

**Design Director:** Tracy Carrington

**Design Manager:** Flora Awolaja

**Design and DTP:** Claire Penny, Paul Montague,
James Thompson, Mark Dempsey

**Photo and Art Editor:** Andrea Sadler

**Illustrator:** Jan Smith

**Model Artist:** Sophie Dean

**Further models:** Sue Partington, Abigail Dean, Harry Foster

**Digital Workflow:** Edward MacDermott

**Production:** Victoria Grimsell, Christina Brown

**Scanning:** Acumen Colour Ltd

Published by Abbey Children's Books
(a division of Abbey Home Media Group)

Abbey Home Media Group
435-437 Edgware Road
London W2 1TH
United Kingdom

© 2002 Abbey Home Media Group plc

Printed and bound by Dai Nippon, Hong Kong

Linking art to the world around us

# artyfacts
# Machines
## and Transport

# Contents

WRITTEN BY John Stringer

# Printing blocks

**B**efore the printing press was invented, anything that you wanted to copy, such as a letter or a book, had to be block-printed or copied by hand. This was a slow process. The printing press made copying much easier.

## PRINTING IN CHINA

The Chinese invented block printing in about the sixth century. By the late ninth century, they were printing books. They carved whole pages of text onto wooden blocks then covered the blocks with ink and pressed them onto paper. This was the earliest form of letterpress printing. In about 1045, the printer Bi Sheng made the first moveable type using characters carved from clay.

## GUTENBERG'S PRESS

Printing in Europe began in 1450, with the press invented by the German, Johannes Gutenberg. This press used a separate piece of metal type for each letter, called moveable type. The same piece could be used over and over again. Gutenberg's press could print about 300 pages a day.

## NEW IDEAS

The early printing presses were worked by hand. In the 1800s a labour-saving, steam-powered cylinder press was made in Germany. It could print over 1,000 sheets an hour. The pieces of type were fixed to a turning cylinder which pressed against paper wrapped around a second cylinder. This steam machine printed 8,000 sheets an hour. Today, high-speed printing machines can print in colour on both sides of the paper. They are often controlled by a computer. Modern printing presses that print from huge reels of paper can produce up to 60,000 copies an hour.

# Potato prints

potato

tissue
paper

plastic
knife

paints

paintbrush

scissors

glue

coloured
paper

Print patterns onto paper with carrots and onions too

**1** Cut a potato in half, mark out a pattern and cut it out.

*You can also make some funny face potato prints!*

**2** Brush paint onto the potato surface.

**3** Press the potato down on the tissue paper to make your print.

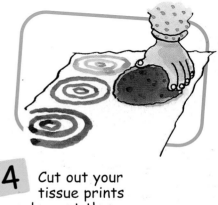

**4** Cut out your tissue prints and mount them on coloured backing paper.

5

# Gas bags

A group of colourful balloons drifting slowly across the sky is an exciting sight. But how do the balloons get up there? The balloonist relies on a steady supply of hot air to get the balloon up in the sky and to keep it airborne. Before the balloon takes off, a fire is lit underneath the opening at its base. This heats the air inside the balloon.

## HOT AIR

The reason hot-air balloons can lift passengers is because hot air behaves in a special way. When the air inside the balloon is heated, its invisible molecules move faster and begin to push against each other, just as water molecules do when it begins to boil. As the air molecules move faster and faster, they take up more space, so the warm air inside the balloon expands. Molecules move around more when they are warm and less when they are cold.

## LIFT OFF

The warm air in the balloon is now lighter than the cooler air outside. The lighter air rises, and takes the balloon, basket and passengers with it. The balloonist keeps the air inside the balloon hot by occasionally heating it.

## GOING UP

Heating the air in your house won't make your house blow away, but it does make the air rise. It flows towards the ceiling, spreading out. When the air cools it sinks back down towards the floor.

# Hot-air balloon

*Why not add some passengers to the basket of the balloon?*

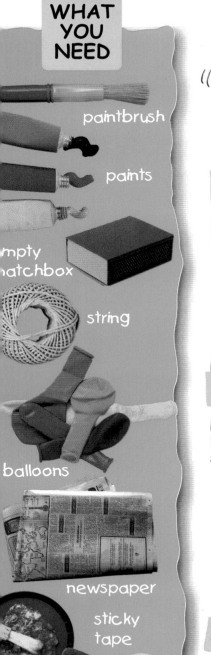

paintbrush

paints

empty matchbox

string

balloons

newspaper

sticky tape

paste

large needle

**1**

Blow up the balloon and knot the end tightly.

**2**

Paste and cover the balloon with small strips of newspaper.

**3**

When dry, paint the balloon different patterns and colours. When the paint is dry, burst the balloon.

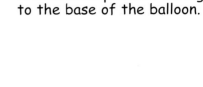

**4**

Paint your box and thread string from each corner, then attach each piece of string to the base of the balloon.

*Thread a long piece of string through the top of the balloon and knot it. Now hang your balloon from the ceiling!*

7

# Skyrails

Monorail trains are not like the trains we usually see. They run above or below the rails, rather than along the ground. Several countries have monorail systems. America's first monorail opened at Disneyland in California in 1957, while a 13-kilometre track was specially built for the 1964 Olympic Games in Tokyo, the capital city of Japan.

## HANGING FROM RAILS

Some monorail trains run along a rail which is strung above them. The separate wagons, known as 'cars' or 'carriages', hang freely from the rail. It provides them with power and acts as a support for their wheels. In the newer 'split-rail' types, the cars hang from two rails which are hidden inside a closed section. This keeps the tracks dry and makes the train quieter.

## FAST AND QUIET

Monorail trains are designed to travel faster and more quietly than other trains, and to use their fuel more efficiently. Some are powered by electric motors, others have petrol engines, and some use gas turbines. The carriage guide-wheels are made of rubber, which helps keep noise levels low.

## BALANCING ON THE TRACKS

Most existing monorail systems run above the track. The cars rest on, or straddle, the track. This type of monorail has a special instrument called a gyroscope to balance the carriages and keep them upright. Sometimes, they also have guide wheels that grip the side of the rail.

# Machines

## Mini monorail

You can make and operate...

### WHAT YOU NEED

- small cardboard cartons
- metallic paint
- card
- paintbrush
- foil
- scissors
- beads, buttons, sequins, paper shapes
- glue
- shoe box
- wool
- tracing paper

**1** Paint one of the cartons with metallic paint and cover one with foil.

**2** Cut windows out of the side, front and back. Stick the tracing paper inside for windows.

**3** Decorate with sequins, beads, buttons or paper shapes.

**4** To make the wheels, glue 3 sequins to each side of the top of the box. Make 2 small tabs from card and glue them on top of the box.

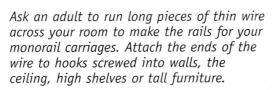

... a miniature monorail system

**5** Thread 2 lengths of wool through the tabs on your car. Poke the ends through the shoe box to make the monorail station. Paint.

*Ask an adult to run long pieces of thin wire across your room to make the rails for your monorail carriages. Attach the ends of the wire to hooks screwed into walls, the ceiling, high shelves or tall furniture.*

9

# Steam engines

The first steam engines were used to pump water and power machinery. Improved steam engines were used to drive the first trains. The trains ran little faster than a horse, but as engineering improved, so did their speed. By 1845, steam trains had reached 40 kilometres an hour and, fifty years later, they were running at more than twice that speed. The most modern steam trains – still in use in many parts of the world – can travel at over 125 kilometres an hour.

## HIGH PRESSURE

When water boils, it becomes steam. Steam takes up much more space than water, and so it pushes, producing pressure. This pressure can move objects, such as the pistons on steam engines. A piston is a disc that fits tightly inside a tube or cylinder.

When steam is squeezed into the cylinder at high pressure, it expands. The pressure of expanding steam on the piston pushes it along the cylinder. Holes called valves let out the steam, and the piston moves back along the cylinder again. A rod and crank connect this pushing and pulling movement to the steam engine's wheels. This is how they turn.

## BOILING WATER

Water is usually heated by burning fuel, such as coal, in a furnace. But some modern steam engines use heat from a nuclear reactor to produce steam.

## Machines

card

silver buttons

lolly sticks

cocktail sticks

bottle tops

nails

metallic papers

scissors

glue

pencil

brush

gold and silver paint

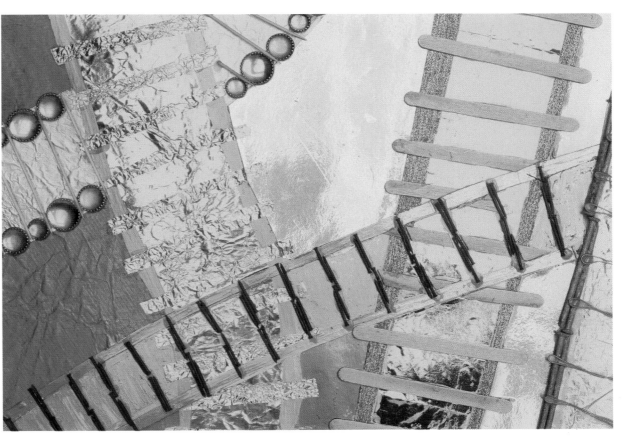

You could add some model trains travelling along the tracks!

**1** Draw train tracks, some crossing each other, on the card.

**2** Fill the spaces between the tracks with pieces of metallic paper and paint.

**3** Use the nails, lolly sticks, cocktail sticks, silver buttons and bottle tops to form the train tracks.

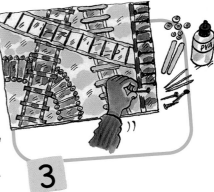

# Bicycles

When wheels turn, they move things. These include machines of all kinds, cars, skateboards, toys, and even giant fairground rides. A bicycle is a simple machine made of two large wheels and a frame. Bicycle wheels help you speed around town, and the only fuel you need is pedal power!

## WHEELS TO TURN WHEELS

A bicycle is said to be energy efficient – it gets you a long way for little work. So how does this happen? As well as two main wheels, a bicycle also has a series of smaller wheels to help it move. The pedals are fixed to a chain wheel. If you turn the pedals once, the chain wheel also turns once. To make things even more efficient, teeth around the edge of the chain wheel fit into spaces in the chain. The chain also passes round the smaller sprocket wheel fixed to the back wheel. So now, every time the chain wheel turns once, the sprocket wheel turns twice, and this makes the rear wheel turn twice. The rear wheel is 200 centimetres round, so with just one turn of the pedals you can travel 400 centimetres – 4 metres – along the road.

## ENERGY SAVER

Most bicycles also have gear, or sprocket wheels added to the rear wheel. The bicycle chain can be shifted from one gear wheel to another by the rider. The different gear wheels change how much power you need for each turn of the pedals. If you are going uphill, a low gear will move you forwards slowly but without having to work hard.

# Wheel pattern

## WHAT YOU NEED

round tapestry or picture frame

nails

coloured thread

ruler

hammer

pencil

**1** Use a pencil and ruler to mark points at equal intervals around the sides of the frame.

**2** Ask an adult to help you hammer the nails in place at these points.

**3** Tie a piece of thread around a nail, then wind it around the 9th or 10th nail to the right of the 1st nail.

Build up threads into a circular pattern

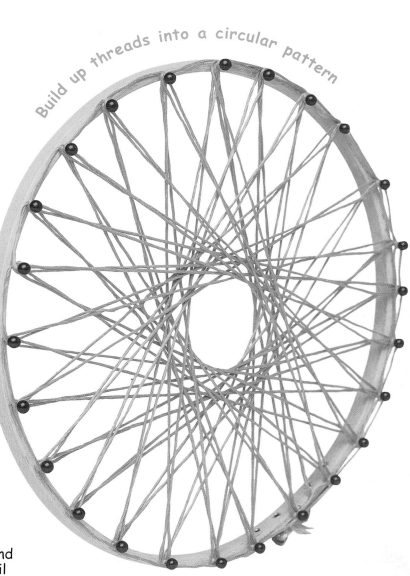

**4** Bring the thread back and wind it around the next nail along from the original. Take the thread across as before. Continue all the way round the frame.

# Windjammers

The windjammer, or clipper, is among the most beautiful of sailing ships. These ships were first built in the United States in the 1800s. They sailed from the east coast of America around the tip of South America to China, where they would load up with tea or spices before returning. They were later used to carry gold mined in America and South Africa. British windjammers also sailed to China for tea, as well as to Australia for wool.

## SLENDER AND FAST

A typical windjammer, such as the Flying Cloud or the Cutty Sark, had a narrow body, or hull, that was deeper at the back than at the front. Large sails hung from each tall mast to catch as much wind as possible. The windjammer was modelled on the famous 'Baltimore Clippers', of Chesapeake Bay in the USA. They were named 'clippers' because their speed 'clipped' so much time off the voyage.

## RECORD BREAKERS

It was not long before windjammers began to break records. The James Baines crossed the Atlantic in just 12 days and 6 hours. The Andrew Jackson sailed from New York around the Cape of Good Hope and on to San Francisco in 89 days and 9 hours. Then the Champion of the Seas sailed 862 kilometres in 24 hours: a distance that was not matched for another 25 years.

## END OF AN ERA

The Suez Canal created a new trade route when it opened in 1869. It linked the Red Sea to the Mediterranean, so windjammers were no longer needed for the tea trade. Instead, they began sailing to Australia for wool. However, in time the wool trade began to need large ships rather than fast ones and soon the windjammers were replaced by square-riggers, which were designed to carry larger cargoes at slower speeds.

# Sail sculptures

Arrange your sail sculptures into a colourful display

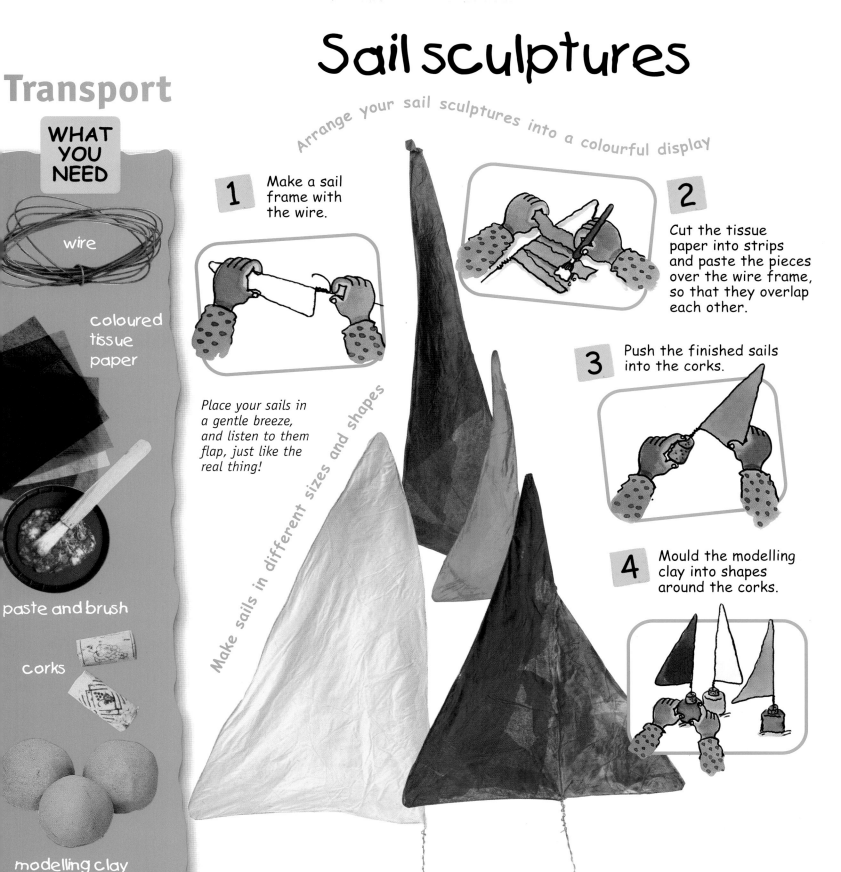

## WHAT YOU NEED

wire

coloured tissue paper

paste and brush

corks

modelling clay

**1** Make a sail frame with the wire.

*Place your sails in a gentle breeze, and listen to them flap, just like the real thing!*

*Make sails in different sizes and shapes*

**2** Cut the tissue paper into strips and paste the pieces over the wire frame, so that they overlap each other.

**3** Push the finished sails into the corks.

**4** Mould the modelling clay into shapes around the corks.

15

# Submarine

We know less about the bottom of the sea than we do about the Moon. That's because the bottom of the sea is very dark and extremely cold.

Tonnes of water press down on anything so deep down. The only way we can explore and map the bottom of the sea is in submarines – underwater ships designed to resist this huge pressure.

### PERISCOPE-VISION

Military submarines are fitted with an optical instrument called a periscope. A periscope is a long metal tube - some can be as long as 20 metres - with a reflecting mirror at each end. It is mechanically operated to move up and down through the water and, once above the surface, it can be rotated to look in a complete circle. So, when the commander needs to know what is happening on the surface, he only needs to peer into the periscope for a full view.

### SUBMERSIBLES

Deep-sea vessels are called submersibles. Their ball shape spreads the pressure of the water over the whole of the vessel's body. Torpedo-shaped submarines cannot go as deep as submersibles because the water would crush them. Submersibles can dive to 1000 metres. They have mechanical arms to collect samples from the ocean floor, and searchlights help the crew to see in the darkness.

### ROVs

Remotely Operated Vehicles have no crew. They are controlled from the surface or from a submersible. ROVs can go into places that might be dangerous for a human crew, such as caves and wrecks. They are also used to repair oil rigs and pipelines.

# Machines

# Mini-sub

plastic bottle

newspaper

glue

bamboo

cocktail sticks

glitter

acetate

scissors

card

paints and brush

**1** Glue pieces of newspaper over a large plastic bottle. Cover the whole bottle and leave to dry.

**2** Cut a circle out of card, make a slit and fold into a cone shape as shown. Glue to one end of the bottle.

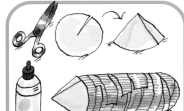

**3** Use card to make tail fins and the look-out deck of the submarine, and glue on.

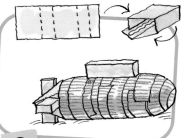

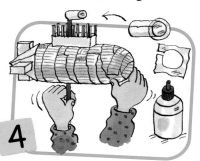

**4** Insert a bamboo stick through the middle of the sub. At the top, glue a piece of rolled-up card to make a periscope, and attach a circle of acetate to the end. Glue stick rails around the top of the submarine.

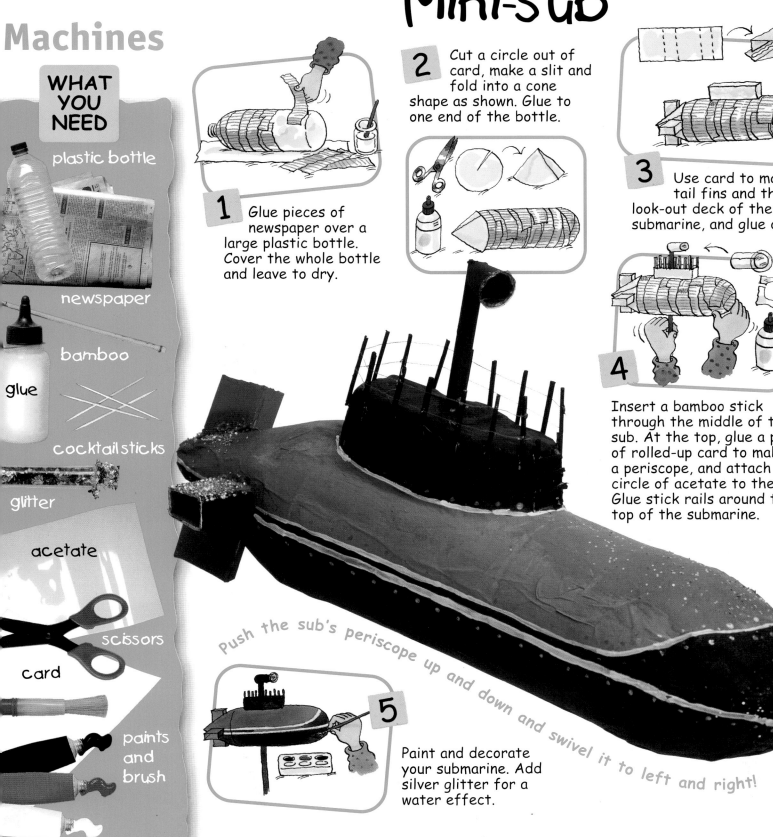

*Push the sub's periscope up and down and swivel it to left and right!*

**5** Paint and decorate your submarine. Add silver glitter for a water effect.

# Propellers

Propellers are blades that are fixed at an angle on a turning shaft. Placed on top or in front of a vehicle such as an aeroplane or a ship, they will help to propel, or push, it forwards.

### THE FIRST PROPELLER
The propeller was invented by an Ancient Greek scientist named Archimedes, who discovered that a turning screw could be used to raise water. Hundreds of years later, his idea was used to build a propeller which could change the turning power of an engine into a forwards movement.

### AEROPLANE AND SHIP PROPELLERS
Aeroplane and ship propellers work in basically the same way. Aeroplane propellers are known as 'airscrews'. The turning blades produce a force called 'aerodynamic lift'. Two or more of the blades are set at the angle that gives the best lift. The blades also help push or pull the vehicle through the air. In most small aircraft, the angle of the blades is fixed. But larger aircraft propellers can swivel to increase the lift, or can even reverse for braking. Most ships have propellers with three or four blades. 'Twin-screw' ships have two propellers, one turning clockwise, to the right and one anti-clockwise, to the left.

# Machines

# Propeller barge

## WHAT YOU NEED

card

pencil

scissors

paints

paintbrush

ruler

glue

small box

corrugated paper

drinking straw

**1** Draw the shapes shown on the piece of card. Cut them out and paint them.

**2** Cut a long, thin piece of card. Score along one edge and fold.

**3** Glue this length of card around the edge of the barge's base.

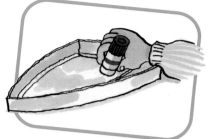

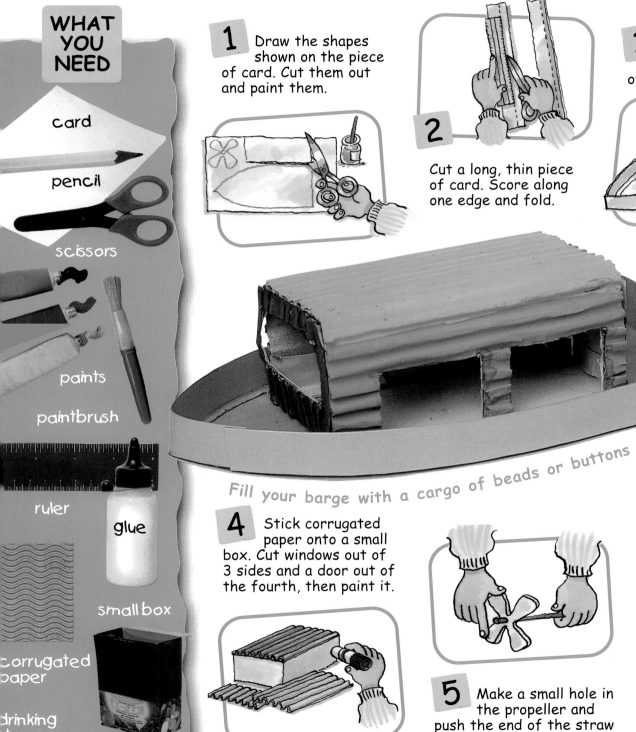

*Fill your barge with a cargo of beads or buttons*

*Cut a small flap from the back of the barge and stick the engine onto it.*

**4** Stick corrugated paper onto a small box. Cut windows out of 3 sides and a door out of the fourth, then paint it.

**5** Make a small hole in the propeller and push the end of the straw through it.

**6** Make an engine cover by scoring, folding and glueing a rectangle of card. Glue the propeller inside.

19

# Speed up!

A fast-moving vehicle needs to be light and have a powerful motor. But it must also slip as easily as possible through air or water. A smooth, streamlined shape will reduce friction, by allowing the air or water to flow smoothly around it, and help it to go even faster.

### STRONG AND LIGHT

Racing cars, power boats and high-speed trains are all light, powerful and streamlined. A racing car is low and wide, so that it slips easily through the air. The powerful ten-cylinder engine of a Formula 1 racing car is behind the driving seat. The driver leans back in order to create as little air resistance as possible. The car is made from light, strong carbon fibre. Its body wings press the car down on the road, so that the tyres grip better.

### HIGH-SPEED POWER

Powerboat motors spin propellers to push them along at top speed. They have streamlined hulls designed to slice through the water. High-speed trains, such as the French TGV can travel at 300 kilometres an hour. Streamlined tilting trains, which lean as they go round bends, go even faster. Made from lightweight aluminium, they are driven by powerful electric motors that get their electricity from cables above the track.

# Zoom pictures

Cut and stick a series of fantastic fast-moving images

**WHAT YOU NEED**

magazine pictures

ruler

scissors

glue

pencil

white or black backing card

**1** Look through magazines and cut out pictures of cars, buses, planes and other vehicles.

**2** Use a pencil and ruler to divide the pictures into narrow strips. Cut these out.

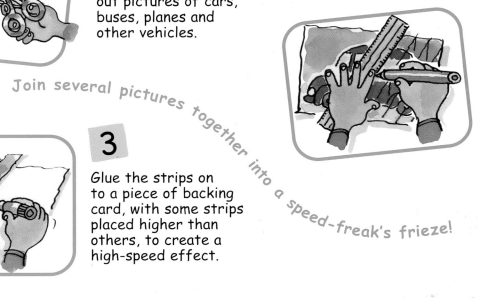

Join several pictures together into a speed-freak's frieze!

**3** Glue the strips on to a piece of backing card, with some strips placed higher than others, to create a high-speed effect.

# Clockwks

*C*locks and watches measure and show us the time. Some have hands that point to numbers on a face or dial. Others have a digital display that changes as the seconds tick away. The parts inside all work together, moving at exactly the right speed to keep good time. Mechanical clocks and watches work because a weight falls or a spring unwinds. Modern clocks and watches use a different kind of energy.

### WEIGHTS AND SPRINGS

An old-fashioned mechanical clock or watch contains a part called a lever escapement. This makes the weight fall, or the spring unwind, at the correct speed. This action moves the gear wheels which drive the second, minute and hour hands.

### VIBRATING QUARTZ

In quartz clocks and watches, the energy comes from a battery. To keep the mechansim at the right speed, the electricity passes through a quartz crystal, which vibrates at exactly 32,768 pulses a second. A microchip slows the pulses to one a second so the clock or watch keeps perfect time. When the battery loses power, the watch will stop. But a perpetual watch can run forever. Inside, a heavy, unbalanced wheel swings when your arm moves. This drives a generator to make electricity. The electricity passes through a quartz crystal and a microchip and drives the mechanism.

# Machines

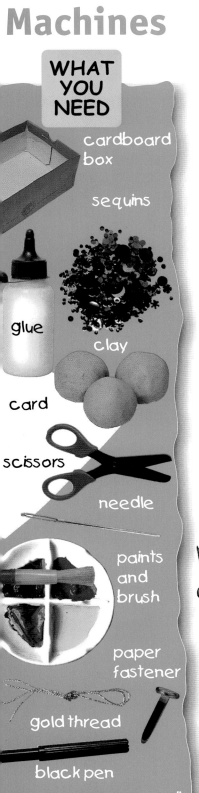

## WHAT YOU NEED

cardboard box

sequins

glue

clay

card

scissors

needle

paints and brush

paper fastener

gold thread

black pen

pencil

# Crazy clock

**1** Draw a crazy outline on card, big enough to overlap your box. Cut out and glue to box.

**2** Paint and decorate with sequins.

**3** Use the pen to draw in a happy face and clock numbers. Cut out two clock hands from card. Make holes in both hands and in the centre of the face. Attach the hands with a paper fastener.

**4** Make a circular pendulum from clay. Attach a length of gold thread. When dry, paint and thread through the end of the box, securing with a knot at the top.

23

# Music machines

You can make a sound by banging a drum. But if you want a tune, with loud and soft, high and low notes, you need a music machine. A piano makes sounds by hitting taut wires of different lengths with soft hammers. When you touch a piano key, the system of levers swings the hammers. A wire then vibrates, and you hear the note. When the hammer drops back, a soft damper stops the wire humming. That's why you can play fast, lively tunes on a piano.

## VIBRATIONS AND OVERTONES

When you play an instrument, you make a vibration. Every instrument vibrates in the same way and makes the same basic notes. What makes each one 'sound' different are the overtones – tiny vibrations on top of the main one.

A guitar and a violin are made in different shapes and materials. So, the overtones of a guitar are different from those of a violin and they sound different. Because an electronic synthesiser produces a wide range of vibrations and can copy the overtones of many instruments, it can sound like any instrument.

## ELECTRONIC EFFECTS

When you press the keys of a synthesiser, it generates vibrations electronically. Filters in the machine let through some vibrations and stop others. This alters the sound and creates echo-like effects to add to your music. You can also alter the volume of the sound and how long it lasts. Everything you do varies the electricity flowing through the machine, thus the sound changes.

## PICK-UPS AND AMPLIFIERS

An electric guitar has metal strings close to magnetic pick-ups. Playing the strings vibrates them, causing a tiny electric current in the pick-ups. This is the signal that goes to the amplifier, which makes it bigger – and louder.

# Cutlery chimes

## Machines

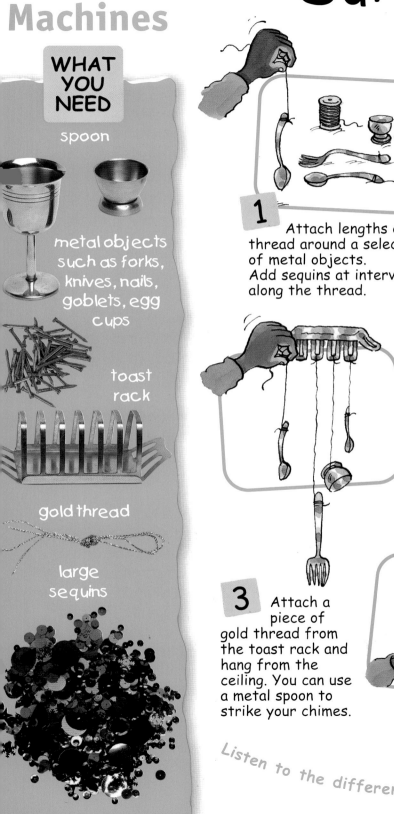

### WHAT YOU NEED

spoon

metal objects such as forks, knives, nails, goblets, egg cups

toast rack

gold thread

large sequins

**1** Attach lengths of thread around a selection of metal objects. Add sequins at intervals along the thread.

**2** Tie all of these to your main piece (in this case, a toast rack).

**3** Attach a piece of gold thread from the toast rack and hang from the ceiling. You can use a metal spoon to strike your chimes.

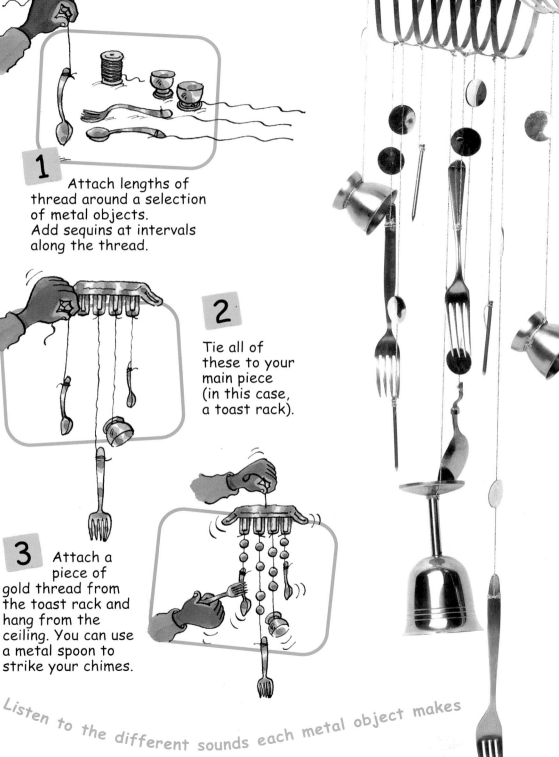

Listen to the different sounds each metal object makes

# Moving parts

Mechanical toys are worked by moving parts, or mechanisms hidden inside them. The mechanisms include motors with gear wheels, as well as rods, cams and cranks. Each part is linked to the next. Together, the parts can make the wheels of a toy car turn round, a model soldier move his arms to bang a drum, or a fierce toy lion open and close his mouth to swallow a lion tamer!

## WHEELS AT WORK

A gear is a wheel with teeth, or cogs, around the outside rim. A gear makes other wheels move. The cogs on one gear fit into the spaces between the cogs in another. When gears turn together they can move a part of a mechanism. Gears can make a movement faster or slower, stronger or weaker, or change its direction.

## RACKS, CAMS AND CRANKS

A rod with teeth on it is called a rack. When a gear wheel locks with a rack, it pushes it from side to side. The arm of a toy violinist may be pushed and pulled by a rack. A cam is an odd-shaped wheel that pushes on a rod. The shape of the cam controls the movement of the rod. As it turns, a cam can push the neck and head of a mechanical toy up and down. It can also lift eyebrows, or raise a hat! A crank is a wheel with a rod attached. When the wheel pushes the rod, you get a sawing action. When the rod pushes the wheel it turns it round. Cranks turn the wheels of mechanical steam trains.

# Spooky pop-ups

**1** Paint a scary night-time scene onto a cardboard box.

**2** Draw and paint a skeleton and ghost and cut them out.

**3** Mould the wire into the shape shown and glue on the ghost and skeleton.

**4** Insert a hole in each end of the box and bend the wire through from the top. Tape up both ends with foil to fix in place.

You are now ready to make the spooky characters pop up!

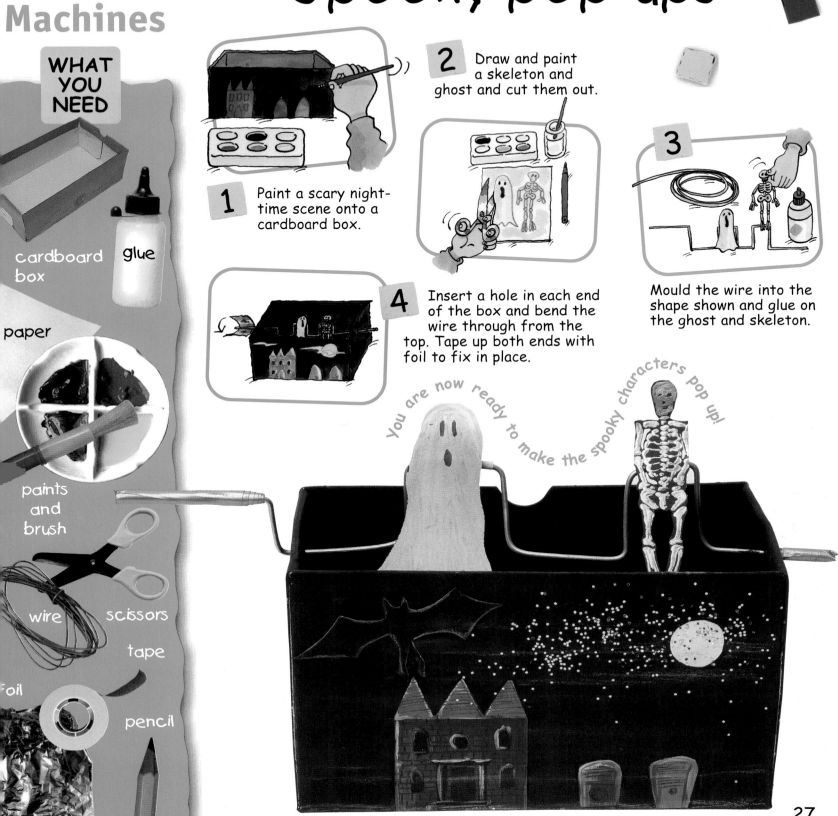

# Weights and pulleys

A tall tower crane uses various pulleys to lift and lower heavy loads at docks or a building site. Pulleys allow us to do more work with less effort. A pulley is really a long piece of cable wound around a series of grooved wheels, then attached to the heavy object. One pulley is useful, but several pulleys make lifting very much easier.

## DOUBLE POWER

A double pulley with two wheels doubles your force, while you pull the cable twice as far. The more pulley wheels you add to a system, the further you will have to pull the cable, but the smaller the force you need.

A block and tackle is a set of pulleys linked together. It is used at the end of the arm, or jib, of a crane to increase the force of the crane's lifting motor.

## LIFTING AND LOWERING

The long jib is supported by a tall tower. A trolley runs backwards and forwards along the jib. A cable runs from it to a powerful hoist, worked by an electric motor. Hanging from the trolley is the hook. When the hoist turns, it lifts and lowers the hook. Because the hook may be carrying a huge weight, there is a counterweight at the other end of the jib to keep the tower balanced. Huge tower cranes are put up piece by piece. Once the first section is in place, the crane builds itself, lifting and fitting new sections. It uses the push of a hydraulic ram, or cylinder to lift itself ready for the next section. If the crane is very high – more than 60 metres – it is often fastened to the building it is helping to put up.

# Cargo crane

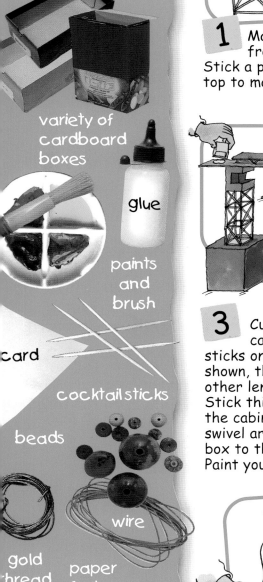

**WHAT YOU NEED**

variety of cardboard boxes

glue

paints and brush

card

cocktail sticks

beads

wire

gold thread

paper fastener

scissors

**1** Make a tower from cocktail sticks. Stick a piece of card on top to make a flat ridge.

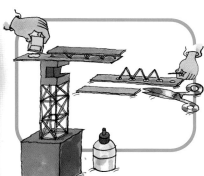

**3** Cut two lengths of card. Glue cocktail sticks on one piece, as shown, then glue the other length on top. Stick this platform onto the cabin to make a swivel arm. Now glue a box to the other end. Paint your crane.

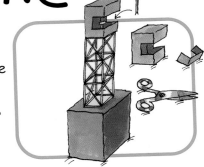

**2** Glue a large box to the bottom of the tower, and attach a small box cabin to the top with a paper fastener so the crane can twist. Cut out a window.

Paint small cargo boxes, stick a wire loop on the top of each, and hook them up!

**5** Stick beads and cocktail sticks together to make a winch, and attach to the box platform. Twist the loose end of the thread around the winch. Turn the handle to wind up your cargo!

**4** Glue 3 beads along the crane's framework as shown. Thread a length of gold thread through the beads. Make a wire hook and attach to one end.

# Jet planes

If you blow up a balloon and let it go, the air rushes out and it shoots forward. This is because the balloon has forward thrust. To keep going, an aeroplane also needs forward thrust. In a jet engine, burning fuel makes a gas, which rushes out of the back of the engine, thrusting the aeroplane forward. The aeroplane's smooth shape also stops backwards 'drag' from the air. Fighter aircraft, like those in the picture, are fast, powerful jets. Passenger aircraft are slower and burn less fuel, but they may use an engine developed from a jet.

### SPINNING BLADES

A turbojet engine has a turbine – a wheel with blades. The turbine turns blades at the front of the engine, sucking in air. Forcing the air through the turbojet makes it light and powerful. But turbojets can be noisy, too. They power fast airliners such as Concorde, and are stored away from the body of the plane, often on the wings.

### WHIZZING FANS

A turbofan is a jet that sucks in air. The spinning fan pushes some of the air around the engine, so that it joins with the burning gases at the back of the engine to give it thrust. Turbofan engines are used on long-distance airliners because they are quiet and use very little fuel. Turboprop engines have propellers spun by the exhaust gases. They are slower and better for shorter flights such as island-hopping.

# Machines

## Paper jets

### WHAT YOU NEED

card

sequins

glitter

glue

scissors

paints and brush

**1** Fold a piece of card in half, open up again and fold the two edges into the centre line.

Fold again as shown. When you open this fold you will have your plane shape.

**2**

**3** Cut the bottom and reverse the fold to form a tail.

**4** Paint and decorate with sequins.

*Fly your planes outside with your friends – which plane can fly the furthest?*

*Experiment with different shapes and colours for your planes.*

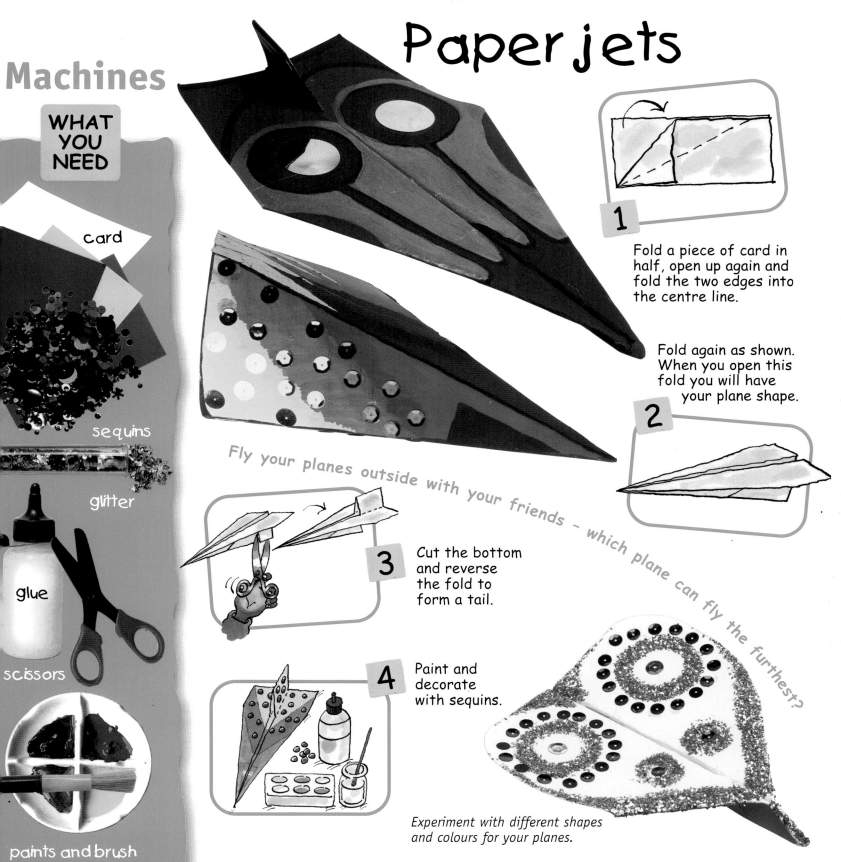

# Wind power

You can feel the power of the wind when it blows. Sometimes it is so strong it can blow you over. Wind power is a form of energy. It can be used to make heat or electricity, or to move things. Two of the earliest uses of wind energy were the sailing boat and the windmill.

## SAILS IN THE WIND

Windmills are built in many different shapes and sizes, but they all work in the same basic way. They usually have two blades with a paddle-shaped sail at each end, making four sails in all. The sails are shaped so that the wind pushes against them, moving them around and causing the blades to turn.

## ENERGY FROM AIR

Windmills called wind turbines are built on towers so that they catch the stronger winds blowing high above ground. As the blades move, they force a wheel to turn. This is connected to a water pump or an electricity generator which will create an even stronger source of power. Long ago, the power made by windmills was used to grind grain into flour. As the wind blew the blades around they moved heavy stone millwheels which ground the grain between them.

## WIND FARMS

Today, windmills are often grouped together in large 'wind farms'. You can sometimes see them on windy coasts or hilltops.

# Machines

# Windmill

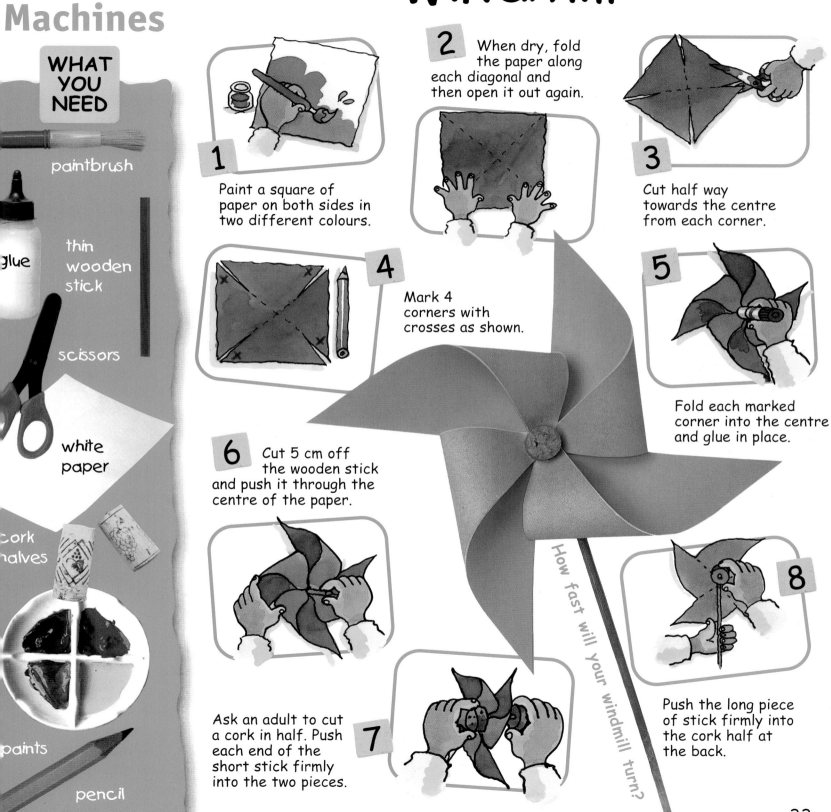

## WHAT YOU NEED

paintbrush

glue

thin wooden stick

scissors

white paper

cork halves

paints

pencil

**1** Paint a square of paper on both sides in two different colours.

**2** When dry, fold the paper along each diagonal and then open it out again.

**3** Cut half way towards the centre from each corner.

**4** Mark 4 corners with crosses as shown.

**5** Fold each marked corner into the centre and glue in place.

**6** Cut 5 cm off the wooden stick and push it through the centre of the paper.

**7** Ask an adult to cut a cork in half. Push each end of the short stick firmly into the two pieces.

**8** Push the long piece of stick firmly into the cork half at the back.

How fast will your windmill turn?

33

# Blast off!

A rocket has to reach a speed of 40,000 kilometres an hour to escape from the tug of Earth's gravity. Most of a space rocket is made up of engine – and fuel. A multi-stage rocket has several engines. Some give it the huge push to blast off from Earth. Others will drive it through space to its target or help steer it. As each engine part finishes its task, it drops off, leaving the rest of the rocket to complete the mission.

### OXYGEN CARGO

Because there is no air in space, the rocket must carry all the oxygen needed for its fuel to burn. The first stage of a rocket, such as the American Atlas V, carries more than 114,000 litres of oxygen, as well as 62,000 litres of kerosene. The Centaur stage above it contains its own engine's oxygen and liquid hydrogen fuel. In addition, tiny Vernier engines are fired to steer the rocket.

### ENGINE DROP OFF

At ignition, the two booster engines help provide a thrust of nearly a million newtons (a measure of force). After a couple of minutes, when their fuel is used up, the boosters are jettisoned, or thrown off. A 'sustainer' engine carries the rocket above the Earth's atmosphere. The Centaur stage then takes over, using its engines to reach the correct orbit. Finally its payload satellite is launched and the Centaur falls away. Space rockets only make one journey. The Space Shuttle is an Orbiter that can make up to a hundred journeys. It rides on the back of a huge fuel tank that feeds over 2 million litres of fuel to its engines in eight minutes, then falls back to Earth.

# Metal rocket collage

**Machines**

## WHAT YOU NEED

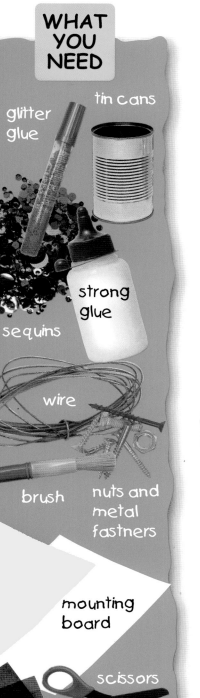

glitter glue

tin cans

sequins

strong glue

wire

brush

nuts and metal fasteners

mounting board

scissors

black tissue paper

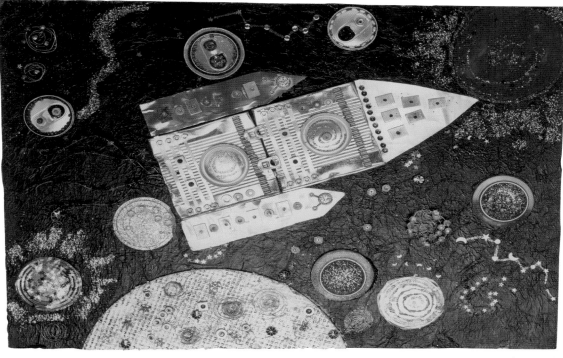

Add constellations by joining up metallic stars with glitter glue

**1** Glue black tissue paper to mounting board.

**2** Squash 2 tin cans flat and stick them on the card end-to-end (body of rocket). Cut out 2 pointed strips of metal and stick either side of body (booster jets). Add a metal triangle (nozzle).

**4** Thread sequins onto pieces of wire. Curl the ends so they stay in place. Attach the twisted sparkles to the base of your rocket, to look like fire.

**3** Decorate your rocket. Stick on tin lids for windows. Add can fasteners and metal strips to make sections on the body.

*Warning:*
*Ask an adult to help with any sticking which uses extra strong glue.*

# Power stations

You can't dig up, or drill for electricity. It has to be generated, or produced from a primary energy source – such as gas, oil, coal or nuclear fuel – in a power station. The primary energy source is used to spin an electromagnet to create electrical energy. Usually, the magnet is spun by a turbine – a wheel with blades that turns when water or steam passes through it.

## MAKING STEAM

Power stations burn fuel to heat water to make steam. Some burn waste, or a product of waste called RDF – Refuse Derived Fuel. Some small power stations can burn wood or even straw, and a system called coppicing can be used to cut wood from trees for fuel, without cutting the whole tree down. But most power stations are wasteful. Only about a third of the energy from the burning fuel is converted to electricity. The rest is waste heat.

## POWER SAVERS

But combined-cycle power stations use the waste gases from the burning fuel as well as steam to spin the turbines. They can produce up to one sixth more electricity. Nuclear power stations use energy from uranium or plutonium fuel to make steam to drive turbines. In the steel reactor core, the fuel breaks up into minute particles, producing terrific heat which heats water pumped through the core. This water then heats more water into steam to power the turbines.

*Biomass-fired power station in California, USA.*

# Smoking chimneys

## Machines

**WHAT YOU NEED**

paper

mounting card

pencil

pastels

oil pastels

glue

paints and brush

**1** Draw an outline of a factory scene, with warehouses, chimneys and power stations.

**2** Use the pastels and paints to colour your picture. Smudge the colours with your fingers for a smokey effect.

**3** Mount your picture.

Add busy little matchstick people to your factory scene

# Robotics

A robot is a machine that carries out a series of tasks automatically. Robots are controlled by an electronic chip or computer, which is programmed to do a job. Robots are used for all sorts of jobs, such as building cars or working in space.

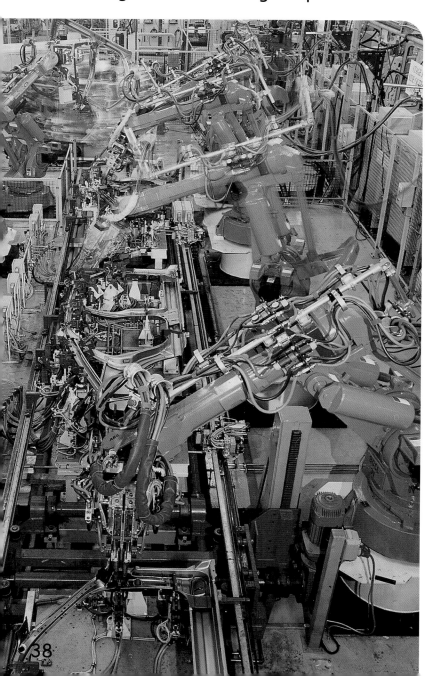

### ROBOTIC ARMS

Many robots are made up of a single arm that can be programmed by a computer to perform different jobs. They are called 'robotic arms'. The 'arm', top and base of the robot can all rotate. They can also stretch to reach different points. Robot tools like these were used in a Japanese factory for the first time in 1970.

### RELIABLE WORKERS

A factory robot carries out a set of simple tasks in a certain order. For example, it will first get the material it is to work on in the right place. It then changes tools and works on the raw material, perhaps drilling it, shaping it or even painting it. The material is then passed along a production line to the next robot. More advanced robot workers use built-in sensors, such as cameras, to help them do their jobs. The advantage of using a robot is that it can work in conditions that humans would find unpleasant or dangerous.

### THINKING MACHINES

By using computer programs, a robot can be made to learn things just as humans do. For instance, a robot can be made to find its way around a maze. This means the robot can 'see' where it is going and is able to avoid obstacles. One day in the future, robots may be built that behave and look just like humans. Scientists might even be able to create artificial flesh to cover the mechanics. Human-looking robots are called 'androids'.

# Shiny robot

### WHAT YOU NEED

paintbrush

scissors

glue

white card

silver paint

glitter

small lid

foil

plastic bottle

nuts and bolts

acetate

pipe cleaners

**1** Ask an adult to help you cut the top off the bottle.

**2** Cut out 3 panels from one side, and stick acetate in the holes to make windows.

**3** Paint the bottle silver. Scatter with glitter before it dries.

**4** Using strong glue, stick on bolts, nuts and foil shapes.

**5** Stick bolts and pipe-cleaner circles onto the small lid to make 'eyes'.

**6** Cut out circles from card and paint them silver. Thread onto 2 pipe cleaners.

*Decorate your robot with lots of shiny bits and pieces*

*Poke the pipe-cleaner arms through the sides of your robot. You can bend them into any position!*

# Moon buggy

It takes a very special sort of car to travel on the Moon or one of the planets. The American Lunar Roving Vehicle, or Moon Buggy, can carry astronauts and all their gear on the rocky, dusty surface of the Moon. It folds up in the storage bay of the space craft for the journey, then it is unfolded to explore the lunar terrain.

### LUNAR VEHICLES

The Moon buggy was first used on the Apollo Mission in 1971. Moon buggies have been used on all three manned Moon trips. To avoid punctures, the four tyres of the Moon buggy are solid. It is powered by a battery that will take it for a 26-kilometre round trip, at a top speed of 18 kilometres an hour. It is steered by a bar rather than a wheel.

At the back are lockers for the tool kit and bags for Moon rock samples. At the front is a camera and an antenna for sending TV pictures back to Earth.

### REMOTE CONTROLLED EXPLORERS

The Russian Lunokhod was first taken to the Moon by the unmanned space craft, Luna 17. Steered from Earth, it visited and sampled several sites, recording and sending back information. In July 1997, the most distant land journey ever was made by NASA's Sojourner Rover, which explored part of the surface of Mars. This tiny vehicle, weighing just over a kilogram, sent over 500 pictures of the surface of Mars back to Earth. A new, bigger model will stay on Mars for a year, and will take surface samples. These will be stored for collection.

# Vikings and rovers

**WHAT YOU NEED**

glue

cardboard box

matchsticks

pencil

paints and brush

card

pipe cleaners

foil

bubble wrap

**1** Create a viking or rover vehicle by glueing together a number of boxes, as shown.

**2** Use lengths of rolled-up card to make tube legs. Glue onto the body of the vehicle.

**3** Draw and cut out a circle. Cut a straight line to the middle of the circle and fold as shown, to form a cone shape for the satellite probe. Glue onto the vehicle.

**4** Stick matches onto the end of a pipe cleaner and glue on.

**5** Paint your vehicle and decorate it with foil.

Make a planetary landscape for your vikings and rovers to roam about on

# Micro-machines

This micro-submarine could be used to explore inside the human body, looking for problems and even repairing cells.

A tiny vehicle could find its way to problem areas and take a look, using a miniature camera. It might even be able to carry out surgery. One day. it may be possible to build computers on this scale. The microchips will be no bigger than molecules – the tiniest pieces of matter. Who knows, we might be able to build a computer as clever as a brain, and the same size as a brain!

Nanotechnology is the science of building micro-machines – machines as small as a millionth of a metre across. An electric motor etched onto a scrap of silicon a tenth of a millimetre wide spins 600,000 times every minute. Its gear wheels are no wider than one of your hairs! It will soon be possible to build a micro-machine that can copy itself, producing new machines as they are needed.

### How small?

Scientists use a scanning electron microscope to build machines this tiny. This kind of microscope can show up and move single atoms and molecules, and even drill holes a nanometre (one thousand-millionth of a metre) across. It could write the words of a multi-volume encyclopaedia on a pinhead!

### Insect robots

Computer-controlled insects may soon be able to go into areas which are difficult or dangerous to enter. Cockroaches with back-pack controls are now being tested in Japan. Micro robot insects are also being developed in the USA. They could soon be used to check and repair inside machinery.

### Repair mission

Scientists are able to build robot machines so tiny that they can travel through the bloodstream to different parts of your body.

# Mini scooter and skateboard

## WHAT YOU NEED

- glue
- matchboxes
- scissors
- paints and brush
- beads
- thick card
- gold thread
- needle
- foil
- cocktail sticks
- pencil

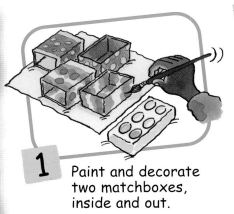

**1** Paint and decorate two matchboxes, inside and out.

**2** Draw the outline of a skateboard and a scooter platform on card. Cut out, paint and decorate.

**3** Cut up cocktail sticks into small pieces, wide enough for the scooter and skateboard platforms. Stick them together, binding them with gold thread, as shown.

*Make other mini machines that fit into a matchbox*

*Make a handlebar for the scooter with cocktail sticks. Poke a hole in the top of the platform and insert the handlebar.*

**4** Thread a bead on each end and secure them by glueing on small balls of foil.

**5** Make two holes in the bottom of each platform to insert the sets of wheels.

# Future cars

The first cars were noisy and smoky, and they guzzled fuel. Modern cars can go further on less fuel, and produce less pollution. Most use diesel, petroleum (petrol) or gasoline (gas) for fuel. But they still produce waste gases that can cause pollution, and may affect climate change. To reduce environmental damage, car manufacturers are looking for new ways to power their products.

## BATTERY POWER

Some electric cars exist, but even they cause pollution. This is because the electricity they use must be generated, or produced, at a fuel-burning power station. They are also fitted with very heavy batteries, which don't hold enough power for a long journey. But electric vehicles are ideal for delivery vans and short town journeys.

## BEST OF BOTH

A 'hybrid' car uses petrol and electricity together. Its petrol engine not only drives the car, but also runs a generator. This produces electricity and charges the car's batteries. When driving around town, you can use the car's electric motor. And on a longer journey, the petrol engine gives extra power. Whenever you put on the brakes, you start a heavy flywheel spinning. This turns the generator, storing extra energy in the batteries.

## FUTURE FUELS?

Car-makers are working on cars powered by the Sun's energy. They run on hundreds of solar cells, but are very expensive to produce. Experiments are also being carried out with hydrogen fuel cells, because hydrogen sends out very little pollution. However there are problems to solve – hydrogen is a flammable and explosive gas, so may be dangerous.

*The solar-powered racing car Sunraycer, manufactured by General Motors.*

# Designer vehicles

## Machines

**1** Draw several 'future cars' on graph paper. Paint and cut out.

**2** Paint a border around a large piece of graph paper and glue on your cars.

**3** Mount your picture.

Draw other forms of future transport – buses, ships, planes, space modules

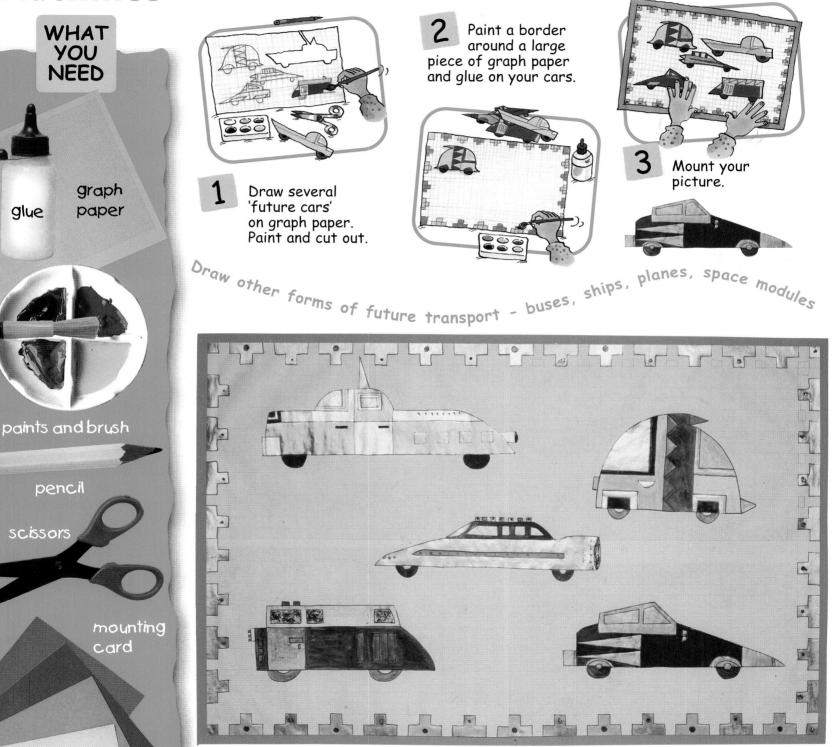

# Glossary and Index

**monorail train** A kind of train that travels along a single or double rail above or below it. 8

**motor** 20, 28

**nanotechnology** The science of building very tiny micro-machines. 42

**nuclear power** A fuel made from uranium or plutonium chemicals. The chemicals produce heat. This boils water for steam that turns turbines, and makes electricity. 10, 36

**piston** 10

**pollution** Harmful waste materials, such as certain gases, which damage our world. 44

**power boat** 20

**power station** A place where electricity is produced from an energy source, such as coal or nuclear fuel. 36, 44

**pressure** A force that pushes on objects. 10, 16

**printing press** 4

**propeller** Turning blades fixed to a boat, plane or helicopter, that push it forwards. 16, 18, 20, 30

**pulley** A length of rope or cable wound around one or more wheels and used to lift heavy weights. 28

**pump** 10

**quartz** A quartz crystal is found in digital watches. Electricity passes through it to make the mechanism work. 22

**racing car** 20

**rail** 8

**robot** A machine that does a job or several tasks automatically. 38, 42

**rocket** 34

**ROV** Initials which stand for Remote Operated Vehicle. ROVs are cars, planes or boats with no people on board. They are controlled by a computer. 16

**sail** 14, 32

**satellite** 34

**screw** 18

**sensors** Parts of a machine, such as a robot, that collect information and help it do its work. 38

**ship** 14, 18

**silicon** 42

**skateboard** 12

**solar fuel cell** A kind of battery that stores electricity made from the Sun's energy used in some cars. 44

**spacecraft** 34, 40

**steam engine** An engine worked by the pushing power of steam. 4, 10, 26

**streamlined** A shape designed to move as fast as possible through air or water, such as a rocket shape. 34

**submarine** 16

**submersible** A ship that can travel under the sea. 16

**synthesizer** 24

**toy** 12, 26

**track** 8, 20

**train** 20

**turbine** A motor or engine driven by a flow of water, gas, wind or some other kind of energy to produce electricity. 8, 30, 32, 36

**turbofan** 30

**turbojet** 30

**turboprop** 30

**video** 16

**watch** 22

**wheel** 8, 10, 12, 26, 28, 36, 40

**wind power** The strength and speed of the blowing wind used to work machines and make heat or electricity. 32

**windjammer** 14

**windmill** A tall tower with blades pushed around by the blowing wind. The turning blades are linked to machinery. 32